Finding Out Who You Really Are

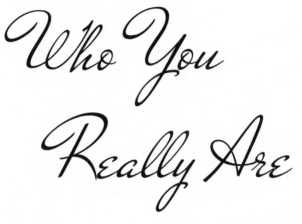

Finding Out Who You Really Are

melody carlson

by design book 2

TH1NK

TH1NK Books
an imprint of NavPress®

TH1NK
P.O. Box 35001
Colorado Springs, Colorado 80935

Cover design by Disciple Design
Illustration: Collins Dillard, Disciple Design
Creative Team: Gabe Filkey (s.c.m.), Karen Lee-Thorp, Darla Hightower, Arvid Wallen,
        Glynese Northam

Published in association with the literary agency of Sara A. Fortenberry.

Printed in USA

3 4 5 6 7 8 9 10 / 09 08 07

FOR A FREE CATALOG OF
NAVPRESS BOOKS & BIBLE STUDIES,
CALL 1-800-366-7788 (USA)
OR 1-800-839-4769 (CANADA)

contents

Introduction 7

About This Series 8

How to Use This Book 9

1 – A Designer Original . . . You! 11

2 – Who Are You? 29

3 – What You Make of Yourself 47

4 – How You Look 63

5 – What You Have to Offer 85

6 – For God's Glory 107

Author 125

introduction

*D*o you ever wonder about *who you are*? Like, why do you look the way you do? Or why you think the way you do? Or where do you fit into this confusing world we live in?

In *Finding Out Who You Really Are* you will find Bible-based answers to these and many other identity questions. You will also be challenged to look and think about yourself in some fresh ways.

Because the bottom line is, *you were not constructed on an assembly line.* You really are a one-of-a-kind creation. And you were designed this way for some very specific reasons. But you only discover these purposes when you turn your attention to the Great Designer — the One who made you and isn't even finished with you yet.

So come along and celebrate your own beautiful individuality!

about this series

The *By Design* series was created to help you experience God's Word in a fun, fresh, and personal way. *Knowing God Better Than Ever* is a great book to start with since it's pretty basic and foundational. The topics of the other three books *(Finding Out Who You Really Are, Making the Most of Your Relationships,* and *Discovering a Forgiveness Plan)* were selected for how they specifically relate to what's going on in your life and can be used in any order that appeals to you.

how to use this book

There are a couple of ways to use this book. You can do it with a group or on your own, whichever works best for you. But sometimes it's easier to stick with something when you do it with friends. And it can be more fun too. If that's the case, you should pick a specific day and time when you'll meet (once a week) to go over each week's chapter together. You should also decide who will take the role of group leader (this helps to keep things rolling in the right direction).

And, naturally, everyone should read and do the writing assignments before getting together. Then when you meet you can go over the chapter, share your answers or questions, things you've learned, goals you've made, goals you've attained, or goals you've blown (no one's perfect). And always make sure you pray for each other during the week. After six weeks, you will not only have completed this Bible study book but you'll feel a lot closer to your friends too.

As you go through each week's chapter, you can decide what pace works best for you. Some will want to read just a few pages each day, taking time to soak it in and carefully complete the assignments. Others may prefer to do one whole chapter at a sitting—but if that's the case, make sure to go back over it during the rest of the week (consider the Bible verses or goals you've made).

Mostly, you need to discover which way works best for you and then stick with it. And hopefully, as you work through this series, you'll appreciate how God's Word really does have meaning and practical guidance for your life.

a designer original . . .

you!

Oh yes, you shaped me first inside, then out;

you formed me in my mother's womb.

I thank you, High God — you're breathtaking!

Body and soul, I am marvelously made!

I worship in adoration — what a creation!

Psalm 139:13-14

*H*ave you ever watched an artist at work? Not just for a few minutes, but from beginning to end? To start with, a painter may make some rough sketches on a blank white canvas. To an uninformed novice these scritchy-scratchy lines may look totally meaningless or even ugly, but the artist has already begun her creation. In a similar way, God was at work creating you when he wove your DNA together inside your mother's body. It wouldn't have looked like much to anyone without scientific knowledge in genetics and DNA, but God knew exactly what he was up to. He knew the details of your eye and hair color, how tall you would be, whether you'd need braces or not, what size shoe you'd wear — he even knew whether or not you'd have a good sense of humor or be able to carry a tune. Amazing, isn't it?

As the artist continues her work, the onlooker may get confused. Perhaps you *thought* you knew what she was doing as you watched her start applying some paint. Maybe you got comfortable with her technique and assumed that a certain object in her painting was about to become a tall pine tree, but suddenly it starts to look more like a scrawny telephone pole, or what you thought was a mountain begins taking on the appearance of a huge pig. And that's when you start to wonder, *does this artist really know what she's doing? Is she even an artist at all?*

And maybe you do the same thing to God occasionally. Like have you ever stood in the bathroom and just stared at yourself in the mirror and thought *God must be crazy?* There's no way he knew what he was doing when he made me — *like this!*

But, like the artist, God isn't finished with his masterpiece — which is *you* — he is still hard at work in you. And he needs not only your patience during the process but also your cooperation. In other words, he wants you to partner with him in this creation. He needs you to stay tuned to him to know how to make good choices and to know how to wait.

Imagine what the artist would do if her canvas suddenly leaped off the easel and said, "You are making a total mess of me! I'm going to finish this up myself." And what if that canvas rolled around in the paint palette trying to fix whatever it assumed was wrong. What a catastrophe that would be!

To criticize a work of art before it's actually finished only shows the ignorance of the spectator. Because creating a valuable work of art takes time and talent. That's why you need to learn to *trust the artist*, to accept that your Creator really knows what he's doing — and that's when you begin to discover all the positive things you can do as you work together with God in designing your life!

> You know me inside and out,
>
> you know every bone in my body;
>
> You know exactly how I was made, bit by bit,
>
> how I was sculpted from nothing into something.
>
> Like an open book, you watched me grow from conception to birth;
>
> all the stages of my life were spread out before you,
>
> The days of my life all prepared
>
> before I'd even lived one day.
>
> Psalm 139:15-16

Getting Real

Okay, maybe you've read some of these Bible verses but weren't convinced. Maybe you're still thinking that God might've messed up when he made you. Go ahead and list three things you really dislike about yourself. (Honestly, it won't hurt God's feelings.)

1. nail chewing habit

2.

3.

Why This?

Do you ever wonder why God allows zits? Or big noses? Or crooked teeth? Or stinky pits? Or flabby thighs? Like why couldn't he have made all of us "perfect"? Why aren't we all tall and thin with killer figures? Why don't we all have thick, luscious hair, full lips, and lashes that go on forever? Huh? What's wrong with that? We could be a bunch of life-size assembly line Barbie dolls, right?

Wrong. God is way more creative than that. And he has reasons for allowing what we perceive as "flaws." For he alone knows what true perfection really is. Do you want to learn how you can trust him with all this?

jordan's story

"I'm sick of me," I tell my friend Kara as we empty out our lockers on the last day of school. It's the end of our junior year, and as far as I'm concerned it didn't come a minute too soon.

"Huh?" Kara looks at me funny. "What'd you say?"

"I'm sick of me," I say again as I slam my locker shut, throwing a strap of my overloaded bag over my shoulder.

"That doesn't sound like you, Jordan," says Kara as she shoves a sweatshirt into her backpack. "What's wrong?"

"Give me a ride home from school and I'll tell you."

Kara grins. "Sure, if you're not embarrassed to be seen in my car."

Kara just got a new (old) car that looks like something straight out of a junkyard or Stephen King flick. Apparently Edgar helped her pick it out, so it kinda figures. But today I don't really care what I'm seen riding in. It seems my life is over anyway.

"So what's up?" asks Kara as she starts up her car, which sounds more like an airplane. "Why is our usually optimistic Jordan Ferguson so bummed? Sad that school's out?"

"Yeah, you bet." Then I go ahead and tell her my pathetic story. "Well, you know I made cheerleader again this year, but today I was informed that I barely made it — "

"They actually told you that?"

I nod. "Not only that, I was told that I need to lose weight."

Kara gets an odd look on her face but doesn't say anything. And this only confirms that she must agree.

"It's true, isn't it, Kara?" I practically scream. "I'm fat!"

"No, no . . . you're not fat, Jordan. But you are kinda short, and I guess if you put on a pound or two, someone might think that you're, well, plumpish. But, honestly, I think you look great. And everyone knows you're one of the best cheerleaders this school has ever had. I mean, you're a total natural."

Of course, Kara would be sweet. But then she's such a strong Christian. Leaps and bounds ahead of me in this area. "Thanks," I tell her. "I appreciate your encouragement. But the sad truth is, I've let myself go this year."

"Well, it was a rough year for you — "

"That's no excuse," I say quickly. "But at least it's over. And now I have almost three months to reinvent myself."

"Reinvent yourself?"

"Yeah. I'll go on a big diet-and-exercise regimen. Maybe I'll even get a makeover."

"Seriously?" Kara looks a bit disturbed by this announcement.

"Seriously!" Dead seriously, I'm thinking as she drops me at my house. "Thanks for the ride, Kara. See ya 'round."

With your very own hands you formed me;

now breathe your wisdom over me so I can understand you.

Psalm 119:73

Skin Deep?

Maybe you can relate to Jordan. Maybe you've wanted to reinvent yourself too. But if you're honest, you'll probably have to admit that you've focused primarily on your *outer* self. Because the truth is, most girls don't spend much time worrying about their inner selves. Oh, they may care about those inner things, but they don't tend to obsess over them. Not the way they do about outer appearances. But do you have any idea why that is?

Whether we like to admit it or not, we live in a culture that's consumed with physical looks. And, unfortunately, it doesn't seem to be lessening. Not only that but the way TV, movies, and the music and fashion industries influence our values, it's just a step above brainwashing. Unless you make a conscious effort to block out all media sources, you have probably been subjected to more than just a few beauty myths. But if you examine these beauty myths more closely, you'll begin to understand that not only are these *not* God's values, they may be essentially nonexistent.

God created human beings;

he created them godlike,

Reflecting God's nature.

He created them male and female.

Genesis 1:27

Getting Honest

1. Write your definition of "a beautiful girl."

Someone who has a nice and Kind Personalaty.

2. Describe yourself.

Blone thick hair, Not very tall

3. Look at what you wrote in question 1. Did you focus mainly on outward or inward qualities? Why?

inward, Becuase someone who is nice is better than how they look.

4. Look at your description in question 2. How does it compare with your description in question 1?

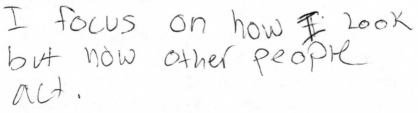

I focus on how I Look but now other people act.

5. How would you like someone else to describe you?

Im nice

6. Genesis 1:27 says that God created you "godlike" and "reflecting God's nature." Name one way that you believe your life reflects God.

His Design

What do you think you will care most about a hundred years from now? Okay, maybe that question totally boggles your mind. Or maybe you're thinking, hey, I won't even be around by then. But consider this: Do you think the things that consume you today will matter in a hundred years? Seriously? Will you be worried about how your hair looks, or whether that guy noticed you, or if your jeans fit right, or even the fact that you possibly blew that biology test? Will it make any difference in, say, 2107?

Now if you can begin to wrap your mind around this kind of thinking, you might possibly get the tiniest glimpse into God's perspective. Time is relatively insignificant to God. To him "a day is as a thousand years." And a thousand years is as a day. God is not ruled by a clock or a calendar. He is eternal — past, present, future, all wrapped into one. No big deal, right? So if time isn't significant to God, what is?

Hearts. God cares more about your heart than anything else. And while your body is a temporary thing, God has designed your heart to last throughout the ages. And he knows that in a hundred years you'll care way more about internal things (the condition of your soul) than about external things.

Ask Yourself . . .

7. When I look over the Bible verses in this chapter so far, what do I learn about me that I'm totally on board with?

8. Is there anything in those verses that I don't understand or don't buy? If so, what?

9. What are five qualities of the way I think or feel or act — qualities that have nothing to do with how I look?

10. Do I spend more time thinking about how I look than who I am inside? If so, why do I do that?

11. What do I think I would really care about one hundred years from now?

12. What can I do today to make me feel better about who I'll be in a hundred years?

Now, let's get back to Jordan. Can you see what's consuming her now? Do you think she'd care about this same sort of thing a hundred years from now?

jordan's story continues . . .

It's the second week of summer break and I haven't lost a single pound! I'm so totally bummed. And that's after I've been eating nothing but Grape Nuts and skim milk for breakfast and green salads with lemon juice dressing for lunch and dinner. And, oh yeah, Diet Pepsi. Plus, I've been exercising. Finally, I told my mom that I have to go to fat camp or I'll die.

"Oh, Jordan," she said to me. "You're not fat."

"Yeah right, Mom." I frown at her slim figure and suppress the urge to scream it's not fair!

"You're just built differently."

"Short and fat, you mean?"

"You're built like Grandma Ferguson."

"Oh, great," I told her. "Next you'll tell me that I'll soon be growing a beard like Uncle Mike."

She just laughed. But then I told her that I was considering doing something drastic like getting stomach staples or becoming bulimic. "Seriously, Mom," I threatened. "I've been studying some websites and I think I can do it."

Well, that got her. And by the end of the week she had found a fat camp with an opening for me. I go in mid-July, and I've decided not to tell any of my friends exactly where I'm going, since I know that they will (1) not get it, (2) try to talk me out of it (especially Kara), or (3) make fun of me behind my back.

Instead I'm telling everyone that I'm going to this fancy spa retreat. And now they're all jealous. Well, except for Kara. She's the only one who consistently sees through me.

"You're going to try to lose weight, aren't you?" she said.

"Nooo . . ."

"Don't lie to me, Jordan."

Okay, I was thinking it's not really a lie — I mean, I am not going to "try" to lose weight. I'm going to go and actually lose the weight. But I didn't say this.

"Just don't leave God out of the picture," she finally said to me. "He's the one who made you, you know, and he's the only one who knows what's best for you. Don't forget to ask him for help with this."

"Right," I promised her. "I'll remember that." And I'll try to remember that. I mean, I know as well as anyone how sideways a life can go without God. And since I asked him into my heart last winter, things have gotten a lot better for me. Well, except for this weight thing. I need to take control of that.

> Know this: GOD is God, and God [IS] GOD.
> He made us; we didn't make him.
> We're his people, his well-tended sheep.
> Psalm 100:3

Change Can Be Good

Okay, so if God *is* God and he made us, does that mean he doesn't want us to change anything about ourselves? That there is never any room for any kind of improvement? Of course not! But before you jump onto some self-improvement bandwagon, before you sign up for an extreme makeover or go under the knife, why not take it to God first? Why not ask him for his direction and blessing? Why not check to see what his Word says? Why not see what some trusted Christian friends think?

And after all that, if you really feel confident that you're getting the green light (from all directions), then you should proceed with confidence, keeping God in the center the whole time. Because when God's in charge of the changes — that's when *change is good.*

Words to Live By

(Consider memorizing one of these verses.)

Now we look inside, and what we see is that
anyone united with the Messiah gets a fresh start, is created new.
The old life is gone; a new life burgeons! Look at it!

2 Corinthians 5:17

Everything God created is good, and to be received with thanks.
Nothing is to be sneered at and thrown out.

1 Timothy 4:4

Journal Your Thoughts

Choose either 2 Corinthians 5:17 or 1 Timothy 4:4. Does this verse challenge your thinking in any way? Write below what those words mean to you.

Acknowledging the Master Plan

So maybe you're starting to get it. Maybe you can actually appreciate how God really is the great Artist who created you — is still creating within you. And maybe you sense that you've impaired his creativity in the past. Were you guilty of heel dragging or complaining? Or perhaps you questioned his workmanship in general and, like Jordan, tried to take things into your own hands. But now you're ready to trust him. You're ready to cooperate with the plan that he's working for you.

So how about writing some specific goals below? Maybe even just one. What practical thing(s) can you do that will remind you that you're partnering with God? Maybe you'll want to write a positive note for yourself on a Post-it and stick it to your mirror. Maybe you'll give God five minutes of your undivided attention on your way to school. But before you pen a single word, why not invite God, the great Creator, to help you?

My Goals Are:

Your UQ (Unique Quotient)

How unique are you? Do you think you can measure your uniqueness like IQ? Well, this test isn't scientific but it's revealing. And maybe it'll help you see outside the box.

13. List your favorite things:

- color
- month
- animal
- song
- food
- TV show
- activity
- vehicle
- weather
- historical era

14. Describe your physical appearance.

15. What is your wildest dream for your future?

16. Describe your inner person, parts of you that only you and God know about.

It's up to you whether you share what you've just written with your Bible study group or not. But the point is, *no one will have exactly the same answers as you have.* It's impossible. And that's because God made you uniquely you — and you are the only one just like you! Why not celebrate your own uniqueness? And don't forget to thank your Creator!

We don't yet see things clearly. We're squinting in a fog, peering through a mist. But it won't be long before the weather clears and the sun shines bright! We'll see it all then, see it all as clearly as God sees us, knowing him directly just as he knows us!

1 Corinthians 13:12

who are you?

Those who enter into Christ's being-here-for-us no longer have
to live under a continuous, low-lying black cloud. A new power is
in operation. The Spirit of life in Christ, like a strong wind, has
magnificently cleared the air, freeing you from a fated lifetime of
brutal tyranny at the hands of sin and death.

Romans 8:1-2

Now that you're beginning to accept and appreciate the fact that God created you—purposely designed you—just the way you are, maybe it's time to find out *who you are*.

Who am I? Have you ever asked yourself that question? Have you ever gotten a clear answer?

Personal identity can be as slippery as a wet bar of soap at the bottom of a bathtub. It's really hard to get hold of it. Some people live their entire lives never fully understanding who they are—or why they are here. But what they may not realize is that *who they are* is determined by *whose they are*. In other words, if you can't acknowledge God's authority over your life, you will never fully understand or ever become all that God wants for you.

Besides having God in your life, there are some basic keys to uncovering your identity. First of all, you need to be honest with yourself, and then you need to be willing to accept your own uniqueness, and last but not least, you need to love yourself.

All right, maybe you're starting to think this is sounding way too complicated. Like why not just take a personality test and get it over with? Better yet, why not simply create whatever sort of identity you think would look good on you? Like pick-a-personality. Maybe you could try to imitate your favorite celebrity's personality. Clone yourself into someone famous like Kate Hudson or Mandy Moore. They certainly don't have it too bad. And as tempting as that may sound, remember that God has already designed you — and he happens to think that your personality is just great. Oh, sure, you haven't "arrived" yet. Who really has?

Okay, perhaps you know someone — someone who does *not* have God in the center of her life — yet this girl seems to have it all. Maybe she comes across as cool and confident and totally together. You think she has absolutely no identity problems whatsoever. Well, other than being a bit smug. But maybe you actually envy her (secretly of course) and wish you could pull off something like that yourself.

But what you may not be able to see is that she has simply created a persona — a thin veneer of perfection that appears to transport her effortlessly through life. The problem with this kind of "identity" is that *it's only on the surface*. If really hard times hit this girl, it's quite likely that she would crumble underneath the crud. And the fact is, eventually most people are hit with hard times. Some get hit during their teens and others get hit later. The thing is, you really find out who you are (or *whose* you are) when you get hit. And if you really belong to God, you can trust that he will use the tough stuff to make you stronger, smarter, and more capable.

Consider it a sheer gift, friends, when tests and challenges come
at you from all sides. You know that under pressure,
your faith-life is forced into the open and shows its true colors.
So don't try to get out of anything prematurely.
Let it do its work so you become mature and
well-developed, not deficient in any way.

James 1:2-4

Who Do You Think You Are?

So you're wondering about who you are . . . or maybe you think you've
already got it figured out. But sometimes we don't see ourselves all that
clearly. Sometimes our perceptions are completely different from the
people around us. Who is right?

Take a person who struggles with anorexia or bulimia. She looks
in the mirror and sees chubby cheeks, thunder thighs, and flab. But
you look at her and see nothing but skin and bones. That's because her
perception is twisted and skewed. And do you know how it got that
way?

It has to do with downloading. In the same way you can download
certain kinds of software into your PC, you can download all sorts of
things into your mind. They can be positive things or negative ones.
Unfortunately most people are better at the negative ones. Say you keep
telling yourself that you're stupid . . . pretty soon you start to believe it.
And then you begin to act like it. But does that mean you're actually less
intelligent than you were before? Of course not. But what difference does
it make if you believe it?

We send ourselves all sorts of negative messages like "I'm ugly" or "no one will ever love me" or "I'm such a loser" or "I'm too fat." And then you start believing these lies. Worse than that, you might even get the people around you to believe them too. And it's not long until it feels like everyone is sending you these messages.

That's what happened to Jordan. And once she arrives at "fat camp," it doesn't get much better.

jordan's story continues . . .

Wow, there are a lot of fat girls here. I try not to stare as I unload my bags from the back of my mom's car. Suddenly I'm not so sure that I want to stay here. I mean I'm not so sure that I actually fit in. Or, here's what's really scary . . . maybe I do.

"You okay, honey?" my mom asks as she closes the trunk.

I shrug. "I, uh, I guess so."

"It's only two weeks, Jordan."

"Yeah, I know." I force a smile. After all, I'm the one who insisted on coming here. And I know my parents already paid for it and it's nonrefundable. "How bad can it be?" I say hopefully.

My mom gives me a hug. "Oh, Jordan, you've always been such a little trooper."

Yeah, right, I'm thinking as I watch a cluster of very obese girls and I could swear that between the three of them they must weigh a ton. I'd like to troop right out of here and never come back. My mom waves from her car and drives off in a cloud of dust.

"Hi," calls a heavy girl who's like about six feet tall. "I'm Cammie. Are you a camper?"

I want to say no and just run, but instead I nod without speaking and then follow this Amazon girl to a registration table where I am given a schedule, a map of the camp, and a T-shirt (size XL) that says, "Bye-Bye, Fatty." Swell.

Feeling utterly hopeless, I pull out my map and trudge up a hill to what appears to be my cabin (#13 — lucky, huh), then I go inside and find a vacant lower bunk in the far corner of the room, spread out my sleeping bag then climb in it. Maybe I can hibernate for two weeks. The next thing I know the blow horn is blasting, our signal that it's time to do something, but I just put my pillow over my head and pretend to be asleep.

"It's activity time, everyone!" someone is yelling from the door of the cabin. I peek out to see Amazon Girl blocking out most of the sunlight in the doorway, but I just roll over and groan.

"You too, Jordan," she says as she thunders across the wooden floor to my bunk. "Time to get up and get going. You can't burn off the fat unless you move."

The next thing I know Amazon Girl is pulling me out of my bag and I'm on my feet. "It's activity time," she says again. "Didn't you hear the blow horn?"

I shrug and look down. "Guess I was asleep."

"Well, sleeping doesn't get rid of the fat, Jordan. Now, let's move it."

So I'm moving it. Right along with the rest of the cows. And as I'm moving it I'm asking myself how I turned into such a big, fat loser?

"Activity time" turns out to be a fat camp version of Olympics. We count off and are separated into ten different teams. My team's country is Turkey and we are the Gobblers. There are also the French Fries from France and the German Frankfurters. Everything seems related to food. And I think that's pretty weird, not to mention insensitive. Amazon Girl says this is because we need to develop our sense of humor. But if you *ask me, a lot of these fat chicks already think they're pretty funny. I am just trying to lay low — and I'm thinking of any excuse to get out of this place.*

It occurs to me that I might be able to break something if I go really hard at these stupid Olympic games. So I run and jump and climb and give every event all that I have (which gains me some friends among my team and some enemies from others since I easily ace most of the events). But it mostly just makes me extremely tired, not to mention HUNGRY! And by the end of the day, I have not one broken bone, not even a sprain. But I do have a big, fat headache!

We don't evaluate people by what they have or how they look. We looked at the Messiah that way once and got it all wrong, as you know. We certainly don't look at him that way anymore. All this comes from the God who settled the relationship between us and him, and then called us to settle our relationships with each other.

2 Corinthians 5:16,18

What About This?

1. Did you notice how Jordan seems to judge people based on their looks (like "Amazon Girl" or the "fat girls")? Have you ever done that? Have you ever been sorry later? Describe the incident.

2. Second Corinthians 5:16,18 says that some of Jesus' followers judged him by his appearance but later found out that they'd gotten it wrong. Have you ever been misjudged based on your appearance? Describe how you felt when that happened.

Your Ingredients

Besides your DNA, that mysterious code that God implanted into you when you were barely microscopic, there are many other factors that affect who you are or are not. Take your family — circumstances like whether or not your parents divorced, or how many siblings you have, or where you fit in the birth order — all this impacts who you are. And then you have your cultural heritage, ethnic background, and relationships with extended family to help mold you as well. Add to this where you live, your type of schooling, where you go to church, your economic status, and you begin to see how many various influences there are on your life.

But although those environmental influences do affect you, science is beginning to show that your DNA (the way God made you) has more to do with who you are than anything else. Well, that and having a relationship with God (although science doesn't readily admit to this yet). The good news is how this eliminates the need for you to make up lots of excuses . . . like if only I was born into a different family, or if only I lived someplace else, or if only I went to a better school. It's as if the playing field has been leveled—like with God in control, everyone has the same chances for a fulfilling life. Of course, you could still play the "if only" game—you could say if only I'd been designed differently—if only I were taller or cuter or smarter or more talented . . . but then you are second-guessing God. Do you really want to go there?

So what are the ingredients of your life? What do you think you're made of? And what do you think God can do with you? The following quiz is designed, not to pigeonhole you into a category, but to help you to understand your own uniqueness.

temperament test

3. Answer with true or false, depending on your gut response. Be honest. There are no right or wrong answers here.

    1. I am unorganized. _____
    2. I trust my instincts. _____
    3. I enjoy being with people. _____
    4. I do things spontaneously. _____
    5. I like solitude. _____

6. I like being the center of attention. _____

7. I prefer poetry over prose. _____

8. I like solving problems. _____

9. I like scary movies. _____

10. I am careful. _____

11. I like art and music. _____

12. I am a planner. _____

13. People think I'm funny. _____

14. I'm always late. _____

15. I do things without thinking. _____

16. I like following the rules. _____

17. I like adventures. _____

18. People say I'm shy. _____

19. I like math and science. _____

20. I take life very seriously. _____

21. I'm a rebel. _____

Consider your responses and see if any patterns or clues to your personality type emerge. And remember there is no right or wrong response. It's just a way to get a peek into who you really are.

Personality Types

There are lots of books out there on personality types and understanding your temperament. And some psychologists, in an attempt to simplify things, have broken them down into four categories. Of course, it's rare when one person falls completely into one category — although we tend to have one that's strongest. But for what it's worth, here are the four basic categories. Don't let their "fancy" names overwhelm you.

Phlegmatic–is easygoing, happy, enjoys life, very laid back. Phleg doesn't get overly excited and can sometimes appear uninterested. However, she usually has a good sense of humor and keeps friends laughing. Consistent, caring, not overly involved, she likes to sit back and watch others. As a result she can be unmotivated or even lazy. But when she joins in, she's competent and capable. She's kind and gracious, loves everyone and everyone loves her.

Sanguine–is the life of the party, popular, talkative. She's warm, fun, caring, responsive, passionate. Sang sometimes speaks without thinking, an extrovert who always has an opinion. Everyone's friend, but not extremely loyal. She lives for the moment, goes with the flow, gets distracted, and isn't totally reliable, but her friends forgive her because she's so much fun.

Choleric–is practical, hard-working, and no-nonsense. She's self-sufficient and will do what it takes to get the job done. She moves quickly, almost intuitively, makes a plan then follows it through. A born leader, Chol's smart and capable, and once she takes her stand, watch out, she'll accomplish her goals through whatever means suit her. She's not very sympathetic or sensitive. She'd rather solve your problems and send you packing. But when you need someone to take charge, she's the one.

Melancholic–is the quiet one. She systematically analyzes herself and everyone around her. Her moods can swing from extremely happy to gloomy and depressed. Mel tends to avoid crowds, or hangs on the fringes as she quietly observes others. She has only a few friends, but she is extremely loyal. She knows how to hide her feelings and make sacrifices for others. She is the artist, writer, intellectual type. Her tongue can be sharp, but it's usually a cover-up for her very tender heart.

Ask Yourself . . .

4. What temperament(s) best describe me? Why?

5. What do I see as the strengths of my temperament(s)?

6. What do I see as my weaknesses?

7. How do I think God could use my temperament?

> For who do you know that really knows *you*, knows your heart?
> And even if they did, is there anything they would discover in you
> that you could take credit for? Isn't everything you *have* and
> everything you *are* sheer gifts from God?
> So what's the point of all this comparing and competing?
>
> 1 Corinthians 4:7

I Am What I Am

At some point you have to start accepting yourself, warts and all. And this does not come easily or even naturally! It's an act of your will, a deliberate choice, a very definite decision. In the same way that you might have to choose to love someone you don't find all that lovable, you must also choose to love and accept yourself.

This doesn't mean you accept the parts of your life where you're blowing it by disobeying God. No, this is about accepting all the facets of your being—your mind, your soul, your body, your talents, your personality—the whole enchilada. You accept yourself for the way that God has created you and you invite God to make the most of whatever it is you have to offer.

What About This?

First Corinthians 4:7 is a good reminder that God's the one who created you, and he's the one who decided what gifts and talents to give you (so you can't take credit for it).

8. Do you really believe and accept this?

9. What can you do to give God the credit for your life?

10. What will help you remember not to compare your gifts to others?

Pen a Prayer

Write a "thank you" prayer to God for the way that he made you. Acknowledge your strengths and ask for help with your weaknesses. Most of all, ask God to show you how to love and accept yourself the way he does — *just as you are.*

Words to Live By

(Consider memorizing one of these verses.)

A devout life does bring wealth, but it's the rich simplicity
of being yourself before God.

1 Timothy 6:6

So let's walk right up to him and get what he is so ready to give.
Take the mercy, accept the help.

Hebrews 4:16

"Don't seek revenge or carry a grudge against any of your people.
Love your neighbor as yourself. I am GOD."

Leviticus 19:18 (emphasis added)

Journal Your Thoughts

Choose one of the Bible passages in this chapter. Write below what those words mean to you.

My Identity Goals

Okay, this is the *By Design* series, and that means making a plan and making it work. It's now time for you to write a specific goal. What would you like to work on in the area of your identity and personality? Do you need to work on self-acceptance by reminding yourself of the gifts God has given you? Do you need to get to know who you are better by reading a book about temperaments or personality types? Do you need to remember to thank God (each and every day!) for making you the way he did? Whatever will help you to get control in the area of identity, why not take some time to write it down now.

My Goal Is:

So, what do you think?

With God on our side like this, how can we lose?

If God didn't hesitate to put everything on the line for us, embracing our condition and exposing himself to the worst by sending his own Son, is there anything else he wouldn't gladly and freely do for us?

Romans 8:31-32

what *You* make of yourself

Even then God had designs on me. Why, when I was still in my mother's
womb he chose and called me out of sheer generosity!

Galatians 1:15

So now you're getting some ideas about who you are in regard to all
those uncontrollable factors like DNA and the family and culture
you were born into. Maybe you're starting to see that you really are unique
and that your personality actually suits you pretty well. But maybe you're
wondering if there is something you can do to improve things. After
all this series is about designing your life. What kind of control do you
really have about who you are and who you are becoming? Lots! There
are all kinds of ways you can help make yourself into someone you really
like, someone you'd like to hang with, someone you can even admire.

Okay, here's the good news: It won't require plastic surgery,
medication, dieting, or even a lobotomy. And it's not expensive. It just
takes some planning and commitment on your part and, yes, it takes
some work. But the payoff is worth it.

You're probably wondering what we're talking about. For lack of a better term, you can call it Soul Sculpting. And believe it or not, it's something you do every day whether you realize it or not. Maybe you're confused now. Like, do you even know what a soul is? For starters, it's different from your spirit. Your spirit is that innermost place where you hunger and thirst for God. It's the holy place inside of you where God, Jesus, the Holy Spirit live.

But your soul, while definitely connected to your spirit, is somewhat different. Your soul consists primarily of your mind, thoughts, intellect, feelings, opinions, emotions — all those inner things that you know are there but can't actually see. And while your relationship with God is what transforms your spirit, you are the one in charge of your soul.

> Tune your ears to the world of Wisdom;
> set your heart on a life of Understanding.
> That's right—if you make Insight your priority,
> and won't take no for an answer, . . .
> Lady Wisdom will be your close friend,
> and Brother Knowledge your pleasant companion.
> Proverbs 2:2-3,10

Inside Out

When you're in your teens, it's easy to focus a lot of energy on your exterior person. As a result, you might neglect your inner person, or your soul. What you may not realize is that your soul actually *affects* your appearance. Take Jordan, she has enjoyed being relatively popular and people are usually drawn to her (she thinks this is mainly due to her appearance — she's not a beauty, but a fairly cute, petite, blue-eyed, blonde). However, if you ask some of her closer friends, like Kara, you will begin to understand that Jordan's appearance is greatly enhanced by her positive attitude and can-do spirit. Not that Jordan's a dog. She's not. But she looks a whole lot cuter when she's smiling and reaching out to others. And that's usually what she's doing. But not right now.

jordan's story continues . . .

It's my second day of camp, and I am seriously depressed. Now, anyone who knows me would think that's pretty weird. I mean, I'm usually the smiley-faced optimist — or so I've been told. But not anymore. Now I am grumpy and, I'm afraid, a bit jaded. I absolutely hate this place. I hate the smelly cabin and musty bunks. I hate the sound of my cabin-mates sneaking food in the middle of the night. And they do! I think they all do. I have no idea how they got their junk food, but I can hear the sounds of wrappers being unwrapped, chips being crunched. And not only does it make me hungry, I think it actually gave me a nightmare last night. I woke up in a cold sweat certain that I was being eaten alive by rats. Great big fat rats. It was totally gross!

As much as I hate this camp, I hate every single one of these fat girls even more. I cannot stand to look at them, talk to them, or even breathe the same air as them. Most of all, I hate myself. And I hate that I've put on weight. More than that, I hate that I'm turning into such a nasty person. Also, I think I'm a total idiot for begging my parents to send me here. What was I thinking???

Not that I still don't think I need to lose the weight. I definitely do.

Perhaps more than ever since I keep thinking that I'm going to look just like Polly (the girl who used to have the bunk over me until I begged her to switch since I thought for sure her weight would collapse the bed and I would be crushed to death). Polly must weigh more than 300 pounds. And the sad thing is, I can tell she's really pretty underneath all that blubber. But, man, does that chick have an attitude — and a sharp tongue.

I've also discovered that not everyone here is obese. In fact there's another girl in my cabin, Lisa, who weighs less than me. I know this for a fact because we weigh in every morning. And that's a lot of fun! The aggravating thing is that Lisa is three inches taller than me but she weighs less, and she thinks she's fat! So, okay, if Lisa is fat, what does that make me? Shamu?

"You two stick-chicks should stick together," said Polly this morning after our weigh-in. "You could teach a bulimia class or start an anorexia club."

"Yeah, right," I said as I looked down at my thunder thighs. Sitting on the bench in shorts, they spread out like two oversized hams. I glanced at Lisa, hoping for just a shred of moral support, but the girl has barely said two words since I met her.

"Don't judge your sisters," said Cammie (for like the hundredth time). "We all have our own weight issues here at camp, and we're here to encourage each other, to work on slimming down as a team."

"Don't let Polly get to you," said Leah, a moderately fat girl. "She's just unhappy."

"Aren't we all?" I asked her as we walked down to the mess hall for breakfast. "Isn't that why we're here?"

Leah nodded. "Yeah, I guess so. But I suppose I'm not as miserable as some of these girls."

Well, I had to look at her closely after that comment. I mean, how could she not be miserable lugging around what appears to be at least an extra forty pounds? "Why's that?" I finally asked.

"Oh, I'd love to lose some weight," she said. "I mean, I'd give anything to look as good as you do, Jordan. Or," she lowered her voice, "Lisa, although I think she has problems. But I've been trying to accept myself as I am lately. In fact, I've decided that I probably won't lose any weight until I can do that."

"How do you know that?" I asked.

"I saw it on Dr. Phil."

"Oh."

So then we went into the mess hall where breakfast consisted of fresh berries, low-fat plain yogurt, and granola that tasted like wood shavings. And no seconds. No problem!

Just as water mirrors your face,

so your face mirrors your heart.

Proverbs 27:19

What About This?

1. Jordan is still very focused on physical appearances, particularly her own. If she was your friend, what would you tell her?

2. Proverbs 27:19 says that your face is a like a reflection of your heart. What do you think that means?

Soul Sculpting

So where do you begin sculpting your soul? It helps to know a little about yourself, your personality, your likes and dislikes. Maybe the last section helped you to start understanding those things. Now remember the computer metaphor — about how you download programs onto your computer to make it operate in certain ways. That's a lot like your soul. You program your soul with things like books, movies, music, friends, art, relationships, theater, TV, computer games . . . basically, just all the things you watch and listen to and experience.

The question is whether or not you're programming in good, healthy stuff or a bunch of junk. You've probably heard the old saying "you are what you eat." Well, your soul is just like that. It becomes whatever it is you're feeding it. So, what are you feeding your soul? Or are you feeding it at all? Maybe it's starving. Or maybe it's getting fat and sloppy from too much "junk food" like reality TV or video games or gossiping.

The thing is, you're the only one who can really control what you put into your soul. And you're also the one who will either benefit or suffer from how you choose to spend your spare time. Why not ask yourself, *what kind of soul would I like to have?*

Getting Honest

So, answer these questions:

3. What do you do in your spare time? List your activities, and try to estimate how much time you spend on each of them. Be honest!

4. Who do you most admire — not for their looks — but because they seem like a complete person to you? What is it you appreciate most about this person?

5. If you could change one thing about your soul, what would it be?

6. When was the last time you read a really good book? What was it?

7. When was the last time you attended an art exhibit, play, concert, or some other expression of the arts?

Try Something New

Believe it or not, you are the perfect age to try something new. Whether it's getting involved in drama, joining a book club, learning to play guitar, or taking a drawing class, there will never be another time in your life that will be any better than right now.

The reason is that you are building the foundation of who you are. You are sculpting your soul into the person you really want to become.

But if you spend all your spare time in front of the boob tube or flipping through fashion rags, you may end up with a very malnourished soul. And you could turn into a very uninteresting person. Someone that no one wants to hang with.

That's not to say there's anything wrong with TV or fashion magazines — when it's not all that you do. But now is the time to try new things, to experiment, and hopefully to discover some surprises along the way. And maybe you're already involved in something that you're really good at, like sports or drama or music or art, but maybe it's time to challenge yourself by trying something new. You'll never find out the things you're good at if you're not willing to try something different. So invite God to lead you and be willing to step out of your same-old-same-old and discover some hidden talents.

Ask Yourself . . .

8. What is my impossible dream? Is it really impossible?

9. When was the last time I did something creative? What was it? How did it make me feel when I was done?

10. What are ten things I'd like to do before my life is over?

> You're blessed when you meet Lady Wisdom,
>
> when you make friends with Madame Insight.
>
> She's worth far more than money in the bank;
>
> her friendship is better than a big salary.
>
> Her value exceeds all the trappings of wealth;
>
> nothing you could wish for holds a candle to her.
>
> With one hand she gives long life,
>
> with the other she confers recognition.
>
> Her manner is beautiful,
>
> her life wonderfully complete.
>
> Proverbs 3:13-17

A Wise Soul

Common sense isn't all that common, and wisdom can be pretty hard to find sometimes. Proverbs (a book in the center of the Bible) talks a lot about wisdom — about how much you need it, how hard you should look for it, how valuable it is.... And wisdom is probably what your soul hungers and thirsts for. Maybe you're not too sure what wisdom really is. Wisdom can come in the form of art, literature, science, or simply from a story told to you by your wise great-grandmother. But the best wisdom comes from God. And the best way to get it is to stay tuned to God. God's wisdom starts with your willingness to obey him, to get into his Word, and to spend time with him — and it can affect every area of your life.

And God's wisdom is all around you. You just have to be willing to see it. You need to keep your heart open to God, and remain eager to learn from him. But here's the funny thing about wisdom — it's very subtle, and often the people who possess the most don't even seem to know it. They're just keeping their eyes on God and eagerly looking toward the next opportunity to learn and experience whatever he's got in store for them.

soul building

- Start a book group
- Go to a play
- Learn to play chess
- Start your own journal
- Learn to play an instrument
- Join the debate club
- Read a classic book
- Go to an art exhibit
- Write a poem
- Take a nature walk
- Listen to a different kind of music (classical, jazz, blues)
- Go to a museum
- Draw a picture

- Take up photography
- Learn to dance
- Try out for drama
- Write a letter to the editor
- Watch public television or the history channel
- Go bird watching
- Plant a garden
- Talk to an elderly person

Words to Live By

(Consider memorizing one of these verses.)

With promises like this to pull us on, dear friends,
let's make a clean break with everything that defiles or distracts us, both
within and without. Let's make our entire lives
fit and holy temples for the worship of God.

2 Corinthians 7:1

So here's what I want you to do, God helping you: Take your everyday,
ordinary life—your sleeping, eating, going-to-work, and walking-around
life—and place it before God as an offering. Embracing what God does
for you is the best thing you can do for him.

Romans 12:1

Journal Your Thoughts

Choose one of the verses above. Write below about how you think that verse has to do with developing your soul.

Soul Goal

Once again, it's time to get specific. If you're really designing your life, including your soul, you need to take some time to make a goal now. Maybe there's something that just occurred to you today. Or maybe there's something you've been thinking about for a while, but never took that first step. Now is the time to write down whatever it is you'd like to do, or perhaps something you'd like to change. What goal(s) will help to sculpt your soul?

My Goals Are:

Soul Searching

Last, but not least, here are the final questions for this section.

11. Your soul consists of your thoughts, opinions, deep beliefs, feelings, attitudes, habits, character qualities, and personality traits. What is the state of your soul these days?

12. Do you know someone with a very cool soul? Someone who you really respect? Describe that person.

13. Describe the changes you'd like to see in your own soul one year from now.

14. Write a prayer that invites God to do some soul sculpting with you.

Good friend, take to heart what I'm telling you;

collect my counsels and guard them with your life. . . .

Believe me, before you know it Fear-of-GOD will be yours;

you'll have come upon the Knowledge of God.

And here's why: GOD gives out Wisdom free,

is plainspoken in Knowledge and Understanding.

Proverbs 2:1,5-6

how *you* look

Don't assume that you know it all.

Run to GOD! Run from evil!

Your body will glow with health,

your very bones will vibrate with life!

Honor GOD with everything you own;

give him the first and the best.

Proverbs 3:7-9

So you've just finished the section on how you can take steps to improve your inner self (sculpting your soul), but how about your outer self? Are you supposed to just let that part go until you look like a pathetic frump? In other words, is it sinful to want to look good? Is it wrong to wear makeup or stylish clothes? Is it a sin to change your hair color or style, or to get a manicure or pedicure?

Not at all! In fact, God wants you to take good care of your physical self—he actually considers your body to be his temple. And if you know anything about God's temple in the Old Testament, you'll understand that he always wanted it to be well maintained and beautiful. With exotic carved woods and stones and solid gold furnishings, his temple was a real knockout. People came from all over just to see it. This isn't to suggest that God wants you to adorn yourself with gold and diamonds, but that he greatly values you and wants to make his home inside of you. Consequently, he wants you to value yourself just as much.

In the same way he wanted his people to care for and maintain his temple, he wants you to take care of your body too. He wants you to look and feel your best. Does that mean he wants you to obsess over your appearance? No, of course not. As in all things, God wants you to find the balance that best fits you. That means you don't try to look like the cover girl of some fashion magazine. And you don't imitate your best friend. You get to know who you are and what you like and you go for the look that is most becoming to you.

And the amazing thing is that when you start finding that look (and you need to know that it will constantly be changing for you as you get older), you begin to feel good on both the inside and the outside. Because it's true that the way you look is a reflection of the way you feel — and vice versa — the way you feel is affected by the way you look.

You've probably watched some of the reality makeover shows like *The Swan* or *What Not to Wear*, but have you ever considered that the most *extreme* makeover comes from God? When you allow God to transform you from the inside out, you really do begin to look different. When you make the daily choice to love and obey him, it not only changes your heart but it begins to show in your outward appearance as well. No makeup artist or plastic surgeon could ever give you the kind of glowing countenance, winning smile, or sparkling eyes that comes from living a life that's pleasing to God. So if you really want an extreme makeover, go to the one who made you in the first place and see what he can do for you.

What About This?

1. Proverbs 3:7-9 says that "your body will glow with health" if you run from evil and run to God. What do you think this really means?

2. Describe a time when you ran from evil and ran to God. How did you feel afterward? Do you think it affected your appearance in any way? How?

Finding Your Unique Style

Now that you know a little bit more about your unique temperament and are planning ways to enrich your soul, consider how you're designed physically (your height, build, coloring, face shape, lifestyle . . .). All these characteristics can help you determine your best personal style. But here's the key — it's *your* personal style. Not your sister's or your best friend's or your favorite rock star's. And the only way you can figure it out is to figure you out. The following quiz might help you to see who you really are when it comes to appearances.

style quiz

Circle the numbers that sound most like you.

1. I care more about comfort than fashion.
2. I love boots! Especially ones with heels.
3. I'm into sports and I love sporty clothes.
4. I like looking different. I shop at secondhand shops.
5. I like looking natural. Little or no makeup and low-maintenance hairstyle.
6. I love color — lots and lots of color.
7. I love jackets and sweaters and belts.
8. I adore fashion. I love purses and shoes and accessories.
9. I like the kinds of outfits that go anywhere.
10. I like to be noticed.
11. I love pastels and lace and flowery things.
12. I love hoodies.
13. I don't care if they're uncomfortable — my shoes are adorable!
14. I like flashy styles and wild combinations.
15. I love delicate fabrics that feel soft next to my skin.
16. I like to wear neutral colors like black and white and khaki.
17. I spend a lot of time on my hair and makeup. It has to be perfect.
18. I like loafers.
19. I don't want to stand out in a crowd.
20. I like animal prints.
21. I love tennis shoes.
22. Baggy is good.
23. I want my clothes to fit me perfectly.
24. I think tattoos are cool.

25. I like plaid.
26. I love looking dramatic.
27. I like soft, fluffy, fuzzy sweaters.

Five Basic Styles

Now look at the Five Basic Styles and see if most of the numbers you circled fall into one of these styles. (The numbers are listed next to each style)

1. **Fashion-Glamour** (2, 6, 8, 10, 13, 14, 17, 20, 23). This style is for the girl who loves being the center of attention. She loves clothes and fashion and isn't afraid to try something new. She likes to experiment with hair and makeup and loves to give her friends makeovers. Every outfit must be just right, and she doesn't care if it takes hours to put it all together.

2. **Sporty-Fun** (1, 3, 5, 9, 12, 16, 19, 21, 22). This is the girl whose active lifestyle is more important than her wardrobe. She likes sweats, jeans, and T-shirts and tennis shoes. She wears her hair casual and goes for a light natural look in makeup. She doesn't like wild colors or prints, prefers stripes to florals, and can be addicted to hoodies.

3. **Edgy-Retro** (2, 4, 8, 10, 14, 20, 24, 26). This style is for a free-spirited girl who appreciates fashion, but doesn't like looking like it. She shops retro and has no problem mixing it up. She likes accessories — funky

jewelry, hats, boots, scarves. She loves looking dramatic and is least happy when someone has on the same outfit as she does.

4. **Feminine-Girlie** (2, 8, 10, 11, 15, 17, 23, 27). This style is for the girl who loves being a girl. She loves pastels and soft fabrics. She likes wearing dresses and skirts. She keeps her accessories delicate (fine jewelry, pearls . . .). Her makeup is softer colors, very feminine. She likes angora sweaters and floral prints.

5. **Classic-Casual** (1, 2, 5, 7, 9, 16, 18, 19, 25). This is a girl who knows what she likes. She appreciates fashion, but it doesn't rule her. She likes her khaki pants and dark sweaters. She likes tailored jackets and crisp white shirts. She's probably slightly addicted to denim and somewhat conservative in her style, but she always looks nice and neat and gets respected for it.

While no one is completely one style, you probably fall primarily into one or two of these categories. And depending on where you live, you may push that style in another direction (like western or urban or whatever). But if you don't see yourself in any of these, that just proves that you're really unique and should have your own category!

jordan's story continues...

By the end of the second day, campers have formed themselves into several cliques. I have no interest in joining any of these groups, which seem somewhat weight focused, if you ask me. All the really obese girls hang together, keeping as far from the center of things as possible. Then there's what I think of as the middle-weight group, and this includes Leah, and I suppose I wouldn't mind being with those girls since they seem the most normal. Then there's the group of girls who don't look like they belong here. Everyone calls them the Rexies (for anorexic). And maybe they are. Lisa is in that group. Then there's a group that just seems to be made up of mean girls of varying weights. Polly is in this group. And this is the group you want to avoid.

"What's your problem, Babyfat?" Polly says from behind me, as I wait in line for lunch. Babyfat is her nickname for me. Hopefully it will never leave this place.

"Huh?" I glance at Polly and try to look as inconspicuous as possible.

"Why are you here anyway?" She says as she and her friends take cuts in front of me. Naturally, I don't object.

Then I make my best attempt at a smile. "I have my own weight issues," I say, parroting Amazon Girl's mantra.

Polly rolls her eyes. "Yeah, right. It's girls like you who torture girls like us at school — where we're outnumbered. Maybe you need to know how we feel, Babyfat." Then she gives me such a big shove that I end up on my knees in the landscaping strip next to the path. They laugh as I stand and begin to pick bark slivers from my knees. Then I just shrug, turn around and head to the end of the line. Like it's no big deal. Like I'm not really starving. But there's no point since there's no way I'm going to try to get my spot back now.

The Rexies are huddled together at the end of the line, and I go and stand behind them. As usual, their group remains aloof, hanging just a few feet away from the rest of the girls. I'm not sure if it's because they think they're superior or are just scared like me.

"Hey, Jordan," says Lisa in a soft voice. This is like the second time she's actually acknowledged me.

"Hey, Lisa." I try to act like everything's cool as I fold my arms across my front.

"Where you from?" asks a very thin brunette girl. I tell her then ask her name and she says, "Mandy."

I nod and look over my shoulder. I feel so out of it. It's like I'm uncomfortable in my own skin. I never used to be like this. Questions beat against my brain. Like why is this so hard? Why did I want to come here in the first place? And why do I feel so freaking lonely?

"Want to eat with us?" asks Mandy as we slowly inch inside the mess hall.

I nod. "Sure."

So it is I find myself at a corner table with the Rexies. And as I watch, trying not to stare, I notice that several of them pick at their salads then rearrange their other foods and drink lots of water. I stare at the food still on their plates, and it's all I can do not to beg for their leftovers, but I know this is against the rules. And how lame would I look if I started cleaning off the Rexies' plates? Besides that, didn't I come here to lose weight, not put on more?

Suddenly I wonder how hard it would be to become like them. Maybe that's why I'm here. So I can study their habits and learn how to be skinny. For the first time since arriving at fat camp, I'm beginning to feel kinda hopeful. Well, hopeful and hungry.

Charm can mislead and beauty soon fades.
The woman to be admired and praised
is the woman who lives in the Fear-of-God.
Proverbs 31:30

What Is Beautiful?

How do you define beauty? Let's say you got a bunch of people together and told them to think about the word *beautiful*. Would they all get the same mental images? Of course not. Some might imagine a singer like Ashanti or an actress like Cameron Diaz. Others might envision Brad Pitt or maybe Ashton Kutcher. And perhaps someone from another generation might even recall the old wrinkly countenance of Mother Teresa. In other words, *beauty is highly subjective.* Or as your grandmother might say, "Beauty's in the eyes of the beholder."

As true as that may be, we still live in an era where certain kinds of beauty are thrust upon us on a frustratingly daily basis. Whether it's through advertisements, music videos, movies, magazines, or TV, we are constantly bombarded with the images that our pop culture defines as *beautiful.* But that doesn't mean we have to agree. God did give us a free will and the ability to think for ourselves. As a result, we don't have to fall into the trap of believing that, say, Jessica Simpson is the hottest thing out there. In other words, we can decide for ourselves what truly defines beauty. But it's not always easy.

Consider how beauty has been defined by other cultures and throughout the ages. Like women in African tribes whose necks were elongated to strange proportions with layers of metal neck bands. Or women whose blackened facial tattoos are considered to be lovely. And how about those plump women we see in old masterpieces with their rounded stomachs and thick thighs (during an era when skinny chicks were considered ugly). There are some cultures that think hair should be long and flowing, while others feel a cleanly shaven head is more appealing. Some women pierce and stretch their earlobes until they dangle on their shoulders. In Asia they used to bind women's feet to keep them tiny. Strange as some of this may sound, all these customs were considered truly beautiful. See how subjective it can be?

Even in our beauty-obsessed American culture there is constant flux of change over what's pretty or not. Take cosmetics — one season the "natural look" is hot and the next season it's all about colors and sparkles. Or we'll have a year where women want flat chests and narrow hips and then someone like J-Lo shows up and the fashion industry is suddenly selling push-up bras and undergarments designed to enlarge your butt. And how about shoes? Just when you think nothing is more comfortable than a Doc Marten, along come spike heels and pencil-sharp toes. Go figure!

Surely we can step back and see the ridiculousness of all this. But too often we get caught in the middle. Too many times we see the promotions of the latest image of "beauty" and we wind up comparing ourselves only to discover that we'll never measure up. But don't worry — it will all change in a year or so because the beauty and fashion industry is driven by change.

And this is where the bottom line comes in. You guessed it — money. If you can step back and really examine our culture's obsession with beauty, you would quickly recognize that commercialism is the monster behind the madness. In a beauty industry that rakes up billions of dollars each year, we the consumers are victimized by our very own insecurities. Flooded with picture-perfect, airbrushed and enhanced images, we are made sadly aware of all the ways we fall short. Consequently, we are lured into going out and plunking down our cash for the latest product that's sure to make us look like the supermodel who's wearing it. Yeah, right.

So if we can begin to recognize that "beauty" in our culture is too often being defined by the fashion industry, or the moguls who profit from our lack of self-esteem, maybe we can step back and look at beauty from a whole new angle.

How about if we look at it from God's perspective. He is, after all, the one who designed us. Isn't it possible that his opinion on beauty might be quite different from our own?

"I don't think the way you think.

The way you work isn't the way I work."

GOD's Decree.

"For as the sky soars high above earth,

so the way I work surpasses the way you work,

and the way I think is beyond the way you think."

Isaiah 55:8-9

What About This?

3. Isaiah 55:9 says that God's thoughts are higher than our thoughts. What do you think God's thoughts are about the multibillion dollar beauty and fashion industry?

4. God wants you to become more and more like him. List three things you'd like to personally ask him in regard to fashion and beauty.

5. Proverbs 31:30 says that physical beauty will fade, but a woman who "fears" (meaning respects, honors, reveres, loves . . .) God will be admired. Describe the kind of woman you would like to be when you are eighty years old.

Just For Fun

what's your bq? (beauty quotient)

1. How long does it take you to get ready in the morning?

    (a) less than ten minutes from bed to door

    (b) about an hour

    (c) a couple of hours on a good day

2. How would you describe your physical appearance?

    (a) not so hot, but it's all I got

    (b) okay, but not model material

    (c) pretty awesome, if I do say so myself

3. How would you describe your clothes?

    (a) boring but functional

    (b) comfortably cool

    (c) only the hottest threads will do

4. How much do you spend on beauty products each month?

    (a) as little as possible

    (b) less than thirty dollars

    (c) way more than thirty dollars

5. How much time do you spend in front of the mirror each day?

    (a) less than five minutes

    (b) about thirty minutes

    (c) hours

6. How do you feel about designer labels?

    (a) Tommy who?

    (b) only if they look good and not too spendy

    (c) that's all I wear

7. How would you describe your hair?

    (a) it's on my head,

    (b) okay on a good-hair day,

    (c) every one is in place.

8. How do your friends describe your fashion sense?

    (a) that I have none,

    (b) that I'm sensible and stylish,

    (c) that I'm a trendsetter.

9. How would you feel if you had to go to school in frumpy clothes and no makeup?

    (a) just like normal,

    (b) a little uncomfortable,

    (c) I'd rather be dead.

10. How often do you work out?

    (a) when I feel like it,

    (b) somewhat regularly,

    (c) religiously.

Scoring: Give yourself one point for every "a" answer, two points for every "b" answer, and three points for every "c."

what's my bq?

0–12 = Earth Muffin

13–24 = Cool Chick

25–30 = Beauty Queen

What's the Point?

It's all about balance.

If you're an **Earth Muffin**, you may need to consider what kind of image you're projecting and why? Is it possible that you've given up on your appearance completely? Do you have some life issues that need to be dealt with? Take some time to come before God and ask him to guide you, and if you need help, don't be afraid to go get it.

If you're a **Beauty Queen**, you're probably spending way too much time in front of the mirror, not to mention too much money at the mall. You need to lighten up and quit trying so hard to be perfect. You may have some life issues to deal with. You might also need to take some time to come before God and invite him to show you what you need — and if it's outside help, don't be afraid to seek it.

If you're a **Cool Chick**, you have found the middle ground. You're fairly comfortable with yourself and don't obsess over fashion trends. You realize you're not perfect, but you're cool with that. Even so, you need to keep coming to God, asking him to help you maintain this balance in your life.

What matters is not your outer appearance —
the styling of your hair, the jewelry you wear, the cut of your clothes —
but your inner disposition.
Cultivate inner beauty, the gentle, gracious kind
that God delights in.
1 Peter 3:3-4

Back to That Balance Thing

So, maybe you're getting all excited about the possibilities of improving your appearance now that you're almost finished with this section. Maybe you've already started planning a massive makeover. But before you do anything, remember to keep it in balance. Remember that God is your personal designer and he can direct you toward finding what's best for you — that perfect balance. And most of all, don't forget about the inner beauty thing — the way God's love and peace can shine right through you. Because that's the real lasting beauty — the beauty that attracts people to you — and ultimately to God. And that's really what it's all about. Right?

What About This?

6. First Peter 3:3-4 is a reminder that outward beauty is way less important than inner beauty. Take some time to rewrite that verse in your own words, and make it specifically about your life.

7. How balanced are you? Write down an estimate of how much time you spend on your outward appearance (clothing, grooming, mirror time . . .). Then write down an estimate of how much time you spend on your inward person (reading, praying, meditating, journaling . . .).

8. If you find you're out of balance, what can you do to balance things?

simple beauty tricks

- Start exercising daily, even if it's just a thirty-minute walk.
- Exfoliate your skin weekly.
- Try cutting out carb foods that contain sugar and white flour.
- Get about twenty minutes of sun (for vitamin D), then use sunscreen.
- Drink plenty of water.
- Find hair products suitable for your hair type.
- Experiment with clothing styles to find what looks good on you.
- Eat more fruits and vegetables.

- Use natural-looking makeup (with a light touch).
- Avoid drinking soda (even diet).
- Eat whole grain foods and nuts.
- Find a sport you like and go for it.
- Discover what colors look best on you (experiment).
- Massage and oil your cuticles.
- Find a lip gloss that smells and looks great.
- Find a haircut/style that fits your face.

Words to Live By

Imagine that God your Father and Creator is speaking these words directly to you!

You're so beautiful, my darling,
so beautiful, and your dove eyes are veiled
By your hair as it flows and shimmers . . .
Your smile is generous and full—
expressive and strong and clean.
Your lips are jewel red,
your mouth elegant and inviting,
your veiled cheeks soft and radiant.
The smooth, lithe lines of your neck
command notice—all heads turn in awe and admiration! . . .
You're beautiful from head to toe, my dear love,
beautiful beyond compare, absolutely flawless.

Song of Songs 4:1-4,7

Time to Journal

Meditate on the verse above. Write about how it makes you feel to know that God really sees you like that.

My Goals

Okay, time to design your life. After reading this section, you must have a new goal that you'd like to pursue. Maybe it has to do with balance and you need to adjust your schedule to include more time with God, or maybe you need to work on your self-image by memorizing some of the verses in this chapter, or maybe you need to change your perspective about what is really beautiful by watching less TV and tossing out some of those fashion magazines. List at least one new goal below.

My Goals Are:

A Few Final Things

Here are a few questions for you to consider. Write out your answers, and be honest.

9. What do you think when you look in the mirror? What do you say to yourself?

10. Do you like what you say to yourself? Does it make you feel good? Do you think it's what your loving heavenly Father would say to you? Why or why not?

11. List everything you are thankful for in regard to your physical body. Not just your appearance, but things like being able to walk or see or hear. See how long you can make this list.

12. Use the space below to write a prayer. Thank God for making you just the way he did, and ask him to help you make the most of it.

> You can tell for sure that you are now fully adopted
> as his own children because God sent the Spirit of his Son
> into our lives crying out, "Papa! Father!"
> Doesn't that privilege of intimate conversation with God
> make it plain that you are not a slave, but a child?
> And if you are a child, you're also an heir,
> with complete access to the inheritance.
>
> Galatians 4:6-7

what *you* have to offer

How blessed is God! And what a blessing he is! He's the
Father of our Master, Jesus Christ, and takes us to the high
places of blessing in him. Long before he laid down earth's
foundations, he had us in mind, had settled on us as the focus of
his love, to be made whole and holy by his love. Long, long ago
he decided to adopt us into his family through Jesus Christ.
(What pleasure he took in planning this!) He wanted us to
enter into the celebration of his lavish gift-giving
by the hand of his beloved Son.

Ephesians 1:3-6

*N*ow you've come to another fun part of learning about the unique
package of you — and this section is a little like Christmas because
it involves gifts! Did you know that God has all kinds of gifts, talents,
and blessings for you — gifts you get to share with others? Maybe you're
already experiencing some, but wouldn't you enjoy a few more?

Do you remember last Christmas? When it was time to open
presents, did you feel a little excited? Okay, maybe you tried to act like *Oh,*

this is silly. I'm getting too old for this, but underneath you were thinking *Bring it on!* And then almost as soon as it's begun, it's over. But did you really want it to end? Would you have said, "No thanks," if someone had offered you a few more presents? Probably not.

God wants you to be excited about the good things he has in store for you. He wants you to happily grab them and shake them with childlike curiosity. He wants you to open them up with unbridled enthusiasm and try them on and put them to use. It makes him happy to see that you love and appreciate what he gives you.

Imagine how you would feel if you bought someone you love a really special present. Maybe you saved for ages to have enough money, then you shopped and shopped until you found that perfect something—exactly what your friend has always wanted. Then you carefully wrapped it and made the most beautiful bow and took it over to your friend and said, "Here, this is for you." And your friend said, "Thanks, this is really pretty." But then your friend just set the wrapped gift on a table and left it there and walked away. How would you feel? Wouldn't you be disappointed and dismayed? You might even be hurt.

It's possible to do the same thing to God. Some people receive wonderful gifts from him, but they don't even take them out of the box. They just shove them aside and ignore them. How do you think that makes God feel? Oh, sure, people probably have excuses, like "I'm too busy right now," or "I don't really deserve a gift," or "What if there's something in that box that could hurt me?"

But God wants you to trust him, to run to him as his beloved daughter, your arms open wide as you joyfully receive whatever it is he has for you.

God's various gifts are handed out everywhere; but they all originate
in God's Spirit. God's various ministries are carried out everywhere;
but they all originate in God's Spirit. God's various expressions
of power are in action everywhere.

1 Corinthians 12:4-6

What About This?

1. What are you really good at?

2. What do you love doing so much that the time flies while you're
   doing it?

3. What's something you do that other people compliment you on?

God-Given Talents

Some of the first gifts that God gives us are those special talents—the characteristics we seem to be born with—the traits he knit right into our DNA. Talents come in all shapes and sizes. Some of the more obvious ones might be musical or athletic or just being extra bright. But there are hundreds of gifts and talents, and God made sure that we all have some.

Okay, maybe you're saying—hang on a minute, I got robbed. God forgot to give me any gifts or talents. Well, that's where you're wrong. Whether or not you can see or acknowledge it, God has given you a gift of some kind. And most likely he's given you more than just one.

The problem with God-given talents or gifts is that you take them for granted. The reason you take them for granted is because they seem to come so easily to you. It's like just an everyday thing. No big deal. For instance, the girl who's really gifted at playing the violin doesn't think much of it—it's just the way she is. Or the guy who can draw anything—he just shrugs it off. Or the girl who's awesome at soccer, but doesn't even seem to notice. But everyone else does!

In fact, one way to discover what your gifts are is to ask someone else. Someone who's honest and perceptive will probably tell you. The trick is to listen carefully and to take this person's input seriously. It's easy to brush off a compliment or to assume your friend is just being nice. But the truth is, that person may see you better than you can see yourself.

And once you learn to recognize and appreciate whatever your special gifts and talents are, you can use them in even bigger and better ways. And maybe when you understand that these gifts are from God, you'll work even harder to develop them into something really amazing.

Natural Gifts

Put a check mark beside anything in this list that is true of you. Then add more ideas of your own.

- ☐ Sensitive
- ☐ Artistic
- ☐ Helpful
- ☐ Mathematical
- ☐ Good with elderly
- ☐ Dramatic
- ☐ Brave
- ☐ Planner
- ☐ Skilled at dancing
- ☐ Healer
- ☐ Animal lover
- ☐ Gardener
- ☐ Speaker
- ☐ Friend
- ☐ Supportive
- ☐ Funny
- ☐ Scientific
- ☐ Student
- ☐ Painter
- ☐ Good natured
- ☐ Sculptor
- ☐ Organizer
- ☐ Good listener
- ☐ Mechanical

- ☐ Friend of nature
- ☐ Compassionate
- ☐ Problem solver
- ☐ Communicator
- ☐ Imaginative
- ☐ Builder
- ☐ Creative
- ☐ Athletic
- ☐ Nurturing
- ☐ Musical
- ☐ Thoughtful
- ☐ Encourager
- ☐ Writer
- ☐ Teacher
- ☐ _____
- ☐ _____
- ☐ _____
- ☐ _____

jordan's story continues . . .

I think I'm an official Rexie now. I've been following my new friends'
examples for more than a week now and have lost three pounds. Okay,
it's not much, but it's a start. I'll admit it's hard to keep up with everyone
because I feel totally exhausted. But at least my stomach quit growling.
And after a few days, I started to realize how rewarding it can be to take
control like this. I just wish I wasn't so tired.

I've observed these girls enough to know that (1) eating anything
with fat or carbs is NOT good—and that includes almost everything,

(2) exercise is your best friend — why walk when you can run, and going up hill or upstairs burns more calories, and (3) if you drink lots of water or diet soda, your stomach will think it's full. Although that doesn't always work.

It's funny, this camp is all focused on things like fitness, health, and nutrition, and yet no one on staff seems to even notice us — or maybe they don't care. We come and go with the rest of the girls, but it's like we're not really here. Yesterday when we were doing some sunbathing at the pool, I asked Lisa if she thought we were invisible.

Lisa laughed. "Yeah, maybe so."

I looked around the pool. Only the bravest girls put on swimsuits and, no matter how hot it is, everyone (including me and the Rexies) covers up with big T-shirts. I'm wearing my fat-camp shirt now — that XL came in handy after all. Now I can see why the fat girls want to cover themselves up. I mean, I want to cover myself up too. But I don't know why the other Rexies wear T-shirts over their suits. I mean, I've seen some of them in the dressing room and they are really, really skinny. Thea (kind of the leader) must weigh about 90 pounds soaking wet. And she's probably about 5 foot 7.

To be honest, I thought this was all pretty freaky at first. But the weird thing is how quickly I'm getting used to it. Oh, I don't think I'm really turning into an honest-to-goodness anorexic, I'm just doing what I can to shed a few pounds before I go home. Already I've noticed that I'm looking better. Although the only place that has a mirror is in the main lodge — that's to discourage girls from obsessing over their looks.

We go to classes too. Some are about nutrition, and some are about things like body image. At first I thought it was kinda interesting, but lately I've been too tired to really focus. But I keep telling myself, the important thing is to lose weight, right? I have to go back to school next fall looking good. That's all there is to it.

Can you see how Jordan perceives herself as a completely one-dimensional person? All she can see is her physical body, and she's obsessing over the delusion that she's fat. She gives no thought to either her soul or her spirit. And if toying with anorexia is not scary enough, she has also left God completely out of the picture. What would you say to Jordan if she were your friend?

Each person is given something to do that shows who God is:
Everyone gets in on it, everyone benefits.
All kinds of things are handed out by the Spirit,
and to all kinds of people! The variety is wonderful:
wise counsel
clear understanding
simple trust
healing the sick
miraculous acts
proclamation
distinguishing between spirits
tongues
interpretation of tongues.
All these gifts have a common origin,
but are handed out one by one by the one Spirit of God.
He decides who gets what, and when.

1 Corinthians 12:7-11

Spiritual Gifts

Now, spiritual gifts are different than the natural gifts and talents we were born with. Spiritual gifts are what God gives us once we give our lives to him. And the main use of spiritual gifts is to help and encourage others. God may have already given you a spiritual gift, or he may be waiting until you are ready. Whatever the case, he wants you to have at least one! (List combined from Romans 12:7-8 and 1 Corinthians 12:7-11.)

- **wise counsel**–ability to listen and advise others with God-inspired wisdom
- **clear understanding**–ability to perceive and explain spiritual truth
- **simple trust**–ability to trust God with childlike faith
- **healing the sick**–ability to pray for the sick and see them being healed
- **miraculous acts**–ability to pray for and experience miracles
- **proclamation**–ability to speak God's truth to others
- **distinguishing between spirits**–ability to differ between what is or isn't God
- **tongues**–ability to speak in a prayer language that God understands
- **interpretation of tongues**–ability to interpret God's message through a prayer language
- **prophecy**–ability to be used by God to speak God's word
- **preach**–ability to preach God's word
- **minister**–ability to spiritually care for others
- **teaching**–ability to teach God's truth
- **encouragement**–ability to cheer and encourage another

- **generosity**–ability to give cheerfully
- **leadership**–ability to lead others with love and care
- **helping**–ability to support, serve, and help those in need

Get Real

So answer these questions:

4. List your God-given talents (traits you were born with).

5. How do you feel about these talents? Do you take them for granted? Why?

6. How do you think you could better use your talents?

7. How do you feel about spiritual gifts? Have you asked God to show you what he's given you? Why or why not?

8. Describe a situation where a spiritual gift might come in handy. (For instance, someone needs help, do you have the gift of helping?)

Just Do It

Maybe you're beginning to understand what your God-given talents and spiritual gifts really are now, but you have no idea where to go from here. The thing is to just do it. First you pray and ask God to direct you, then you roll up your sleeves and get in there and start using whatever it is that God's given you to do, whatever it is that he's asking you to do. It might be something as simple as changing diapers in the church nursery. Or it might be to start a lunch-group Bible study in your school. God only knows what he has in store for you. But the amazing thing is, as soon as you start using your gifts, your gifts will begin to grow and improve. Oh, that doesn't mean you won't blow it. You probably will. But give your failures to God and ask him to help you to learn from your mistakes. And then just keep on going. Again and again and again.

9. List three opportunities that you can imagine popping up in your life where you might use a gift to help someone:

1.

2.

3.

If you preach, just preach God's Message, nothing else;

if you help, just help, don't take over;

if you teach, stick to your teaching;

if you give encouraging guidance, be careful that you don't get bossy;

if you're put in charge, don't manipulate;

if you're called to give aid to people in distress,

keep your eyes open and be quick to respond;

if you work with the disadvantaged, don't let yourself

get irritated with them or depressed by them.

Keep a smile on your face.

Romans 12:6-8

Spiritual Fruits

Galatians 5:22-23 promises that when you love and obey God, he will bless you with another kind of gift. Some people call these *spiritual fruits*.

But when you stay close to God (the same way a branch sticks to the tree), you can't help but grow these special kinds of fruit. And the great thing about these fruits is that you can and should have more than one and hopefully someday you'll have them all. Look at the list below and rank yourself using 1–5 scale on which fruits you feel the strongest in. (1 = barely visible, 2 = tiny bud, 3 = small and green, 4 = nearly ripe, 5 = bring on the harvest!

- ☐ Love
- ☐ Joy
- ☐ Peace
- ☐ Patience
- ☐ Gentleness
- ☐ Goodness
- ☐ Faith
- ☐ Meekness
- ☐ Self-control

jordan's story continues . . .

I'm having a hard time sleeping. Not because of the midnight "rats," since Amazon Girl found out about the forbidden snacks and did a complete cabin check, which resulted in our cabin being humiliated when she made us carry down bags of Cheetos and Doritos and Ding-Dongs and Ho-Hos and whatever . . . down to the campfire where we all took turns throwing items into the fire. It was supposed to be symbolic, but I think it just made everyone hungry.

I'm not sure why I'm not sleeping at night, but I suspect it's because I feel like I'm starving to death. I have these horrible dreams — mostly food related — and then I wake up and feel all shaky and my heart's pounding and I get all freaked like I'm actually going to die. Then I promise myself that I'll go back to regular eating first thing tomorrow. I swear off this whole crazy anorexia thing and even beg God to help me survive the night. But then daylight comes and I'm hanging with the Rexies again, and I just keep playing their little game.

So anyway, here I am lying on my top bunk where the air is hot and humid and I think I can hear something besides the fast thump-thump of my own pulse that is pounding in my eardrums. I sit up and try to listen, and it sounds like someone is actually gasping for air. Imagining that Polly is choking on a Twinkie that she somehow managed to hide from Amazon Girl, I leap from my bed and go over to see if I can help.

But it's Lisa, not Polly, and she seems to be having a problem. "Lisa?" I whisper, thinking maybe she's just having a nightmare. "Are you okay?"

Then her eyes open wide and she shakes her head no. I reach up to touch her forehead and it's clammy and cold. And then she just starts shaking.

"Wake up!" I yell as I turn on the overhead lights. I can hear girls complaining and grumbling, but I don't care. "It's an emergency!" I scream. "Someone call 911! Now!"

One of the girls takes off yelling "Someone, call 911! Call 911!" And suddenly I realize that Lisa is in serious trouble. In the stark overhead light I can see that her skin is deathly pale and she doesn't seem to be breathing. "Help me!" I yell to Polly who is now standing behind me. "Get her on the floor. I know CPR!"

Within seconds we have Lisa on the floor, and amazingly I can remember all the CPR steps that I learned in lifesaving class last summer when I was a lifeguard at the pool. I pray as I go through the steps, again *and again, but I don't stop working on her. I know that I have to keep this going until help arrives.*

"You're doing good," says Amazon Girl from behind me. "Keep it up, Jordan."

And so I do. Finally the camp doctor arrives and takes over with some real medical equipment. I feel slightly dazed and hurt as I am pushed aside. But I am also exhausted. I fall down to my knees next to Lisa, I take her hand in mine, and I really start to pray.

"Dear God," I say out loud, "please help Lisa. Keep her alive. Please, take care of her, Lord. Keep her going until help arrives and . . . " On and on I ramble, hardly even knowing what I'm praying. But everyone in the cabin is very quiet. And I hear a few girls even saying amen and adding their own one-line prayers. And then the paramedics come in, and everyone who's not of medical assistance is told to get out of the cabin. Although I want to stay, I know I have to get out of their way. So I go outside and continue to pray. But as I pray there are tears streaking down my cheeks, and I am shaking uncontrollably.

"Here," says Polly as she wraps a blanket around my shoulders. "You look like you're freezing to death."

I thank her and pull the blanket tighter.

"Great job in there," says Amazon Girl. "I was trained in CPR, but I swear my mind just went totally blank."

"Yeah," says Leah. "You were amazing, Jordan. You must be exhausted."

Then the paramedics are taking Lisa out of the cabin on a gurney. I look at her as they pass by and she still looks pale, unconscious. "I'm still praying for you, Lisa!" I yell, although I don't know if she can hear anything. And then I close my eyes and I really pray.

Doing Your Part

Sometimes it's hard to know just how to use your gifts and natural talents. Or maybe you're worried that it might all be going to waste. But you shouldn't get too freaked about it. Just ask God to lead you. And trust his timing. The thing is, when you need your gifts or talents, you know they are there. It's not like you have to go out drumming up business. But you do need to be ready. And there may be something you can do that will better prepare you to use your gifts and talents. It could be taking a class or reading a book or just spending time with God. Ask God to show you ways that will prepare you.

gifts in action

- Actively participate in your youth group.
- Volunteer at a soup kitchen.
- Make an effort to read and understand God's Word.
- Start a Bible study group.
- Offer to help with the younger kids at church.
- Volunteer at a senior center.
- Help support a foreign missionary.
- Visit sick people in the hospital.
- Write letters to overseas servicemen and women.
- Get involved in an outreach ministry.
- Pray for the leaders in your community.
- Be a friend to someone in need.

Words to Live By

In this way we are like the various parts of a human body. Each
part gets its meaning from the body as a whole,
not the other way around. The body we're talking about is Christ's
body of chosen people. Each of us finds our meaning and
function as a part of his body. But as a chopped-off finger or cut-
off toe we wouldn't amount to much, would we?
So since we find ourselves fashioned into all these excellently
formed and marvelously functioning parts in Christ's body, let's just
go ahead and be what we were made to be, without enviously
or pridefully comparing ourselves with each other, or trying to be
something we aren't.

Romans 12:4-6

Journal Your Thoughts

Consider the verse above. Write what those words mean to you personally.

My Gift Goals

It's time to get specific with the direction you feel God is leading you in regard to your gifts and talents. You've probably had more than a couple of ideas by now. Go ahead and write down your new goals.

My Goals Are:

Final Thoughts on Gifts

Answer the following questions:

10. How do I feel about actually using my spiritual gifts? Am I excited, intimidated, or uninterested? Why?

11. If I could pick another spiritual gift, I would choose _____ _____. Why?

12. Use the space below to write a thank-you prayer for your gifts and natural talents.

But what happens when we live God's way?
He brings gifts into our lives, much the same way that fruit appears
in an orchard—things like affection for others,
exuberance about life, serenity.
We develop a willingness to stick with things, a sense of
compassion in the heart, and a conviction that a basic
holiness permeates things and people.
We find ourselves involved in loyal commitments, not needing to
force our way in life, able to marshal and direct our energies wisely.
Legalism is helpless in bringing this about; it only gets in the way.
Galatians 5:22-23

for *God's* glory

Now God has us where he wants us,

with all the time in this world and the next to shower

grace and kindness upon us in Christ Jesus.

Saving is all his idea, and all his work.

All we do is trust him enough to let him do it.

It's God's gift from start to finish!

We don't play the major role.

If we did, we'd probably go around bragging

that we'd done the whole thing!

No, we neither make nor save ourselves.

God does both the making and saving.

He creates each of us by Christ Jesus to join him in the work he does,

the good work he has gotten ready for us to do,

work we had better be doing.

Ephesians 2:7-10

Do you know that God has good reason for making you just the way
he did. But did you know that he designed you for himself as well?
First, he made you with the capacity to become his beloved child and

close friend. And he wants to enjoy a relationship with you. That's why he designed you with the ability to love and forgive in the same way that he loves and forgives you. That ensures that your friendship with God will be ongoing.

But he also made you with the potential to reach out to certain people — people who need *someone just like you* in their lives. And he'll put you in the place to do that — if you're willing and obedient to him, because God wants you to partner with him in his nonstop task of showing mercy to everyone. He wants your life so full of his love that you can't help but overflow onto others.

Think about the Christians who've impacted your life . . . chances are they are people who were sold out for God — people whose passion was contagious, or at least interesting enough to make you take a second look. Maybe it was someone who loved the unlovely. Or maybe it was someone who showed mercy when mercy was undeserved. That's the kind of person God wants you to be — someone whose sincerity, love, and gracious spirit causes others to stop and take notice.

Love from the center of who you are; don't fake it.
Run for dear life from evil; hold on for dear life to good.
Be good friends who love deeply; practice playing second fiddle.
Don't burn out; keep yourselves fueled and aflame.
Be alert servants of the Master, cheerfully expectant.
Don't quit in hard times; pray all the harder.
Help needy Christians; be inventive in hospitality.

Romans 12:9-13

What About This?

1. Ephesians 2:7 says that God has you where he wants you, meaning that it's no coincidence that you live where you do and are surrounded by the people in your life. But what do you think he wants you to do about it? What's one thing you could do today to bring God glory?

2. Romans 12:9 says to love from your heart and not to fake it. List three people you believe God wants you to love with this kind of genuine sincerity and ask him to help you do it.

3. Romans 12:13 says to help needy Christians and be creative in hospitality. List one specific thing you could do to make that verse real in your life.

Pure Motives

Does this mean that you please God by doing lots of "good" stuff? That you get his attention by putting on a "good" act? Or by doing a bunch of "good" works? Some people fall into this "do good" trap. They think that they can work their way into God's favor by acting "just right." And that's where legalism is born. But Jesus gave his life to free us from this kind of legalistic religious thinking. He wants us to simply enjoy a healthy relationship with God — and that should be the motivation for doing "good" things. But the cool part is that you probably won't always know when you're doing something God considers "good." You'll just be living out your everyday life and trying to keep him first. That's when you not only make God happy, but you make others sit up and take notice.

jordan's story continues . . .

Everyone at camp has heard the news by now. Lisa suffered a cardiac arrest last night — it could've killed her. Amazon Girl informed us this morning that Lisa was released from ICU and is in stable condition. I'm so thankful. And I can't help but think God has something to do with it. I plan to write her a card today, saying just that.

Naturally, everyone at camp, including me, assumes Lisa's medical emergency was a result from her being anorexic. Well, everyone except the other Rexies. They're still not so sure.

"How can you know that, Jordan?" Thea questions me at breakfast. "What makes you such an expert on anorexia anyway? Have you checked out the websites? Have you really researched this whole thing like I have?"

I shake my head and look down at my bowl of granola. Then with a feeling of defiance, I reach for the pitcher of skim milk and pour it on. I am going to eat today! I reach for the untouched bowl of fruit and toss some melon and strawberries on top.

"Lisa might've had some preexisting medical condition," says Thea, like she's unwilling to give this up without a fight. "It's entirely possible that she was born with a defective heart."

"I suppose it's possible," I say as I take a big spoonful of what suddenly looks like mouth-watering granola. As I'm crunching on the whole grains and nuts, I watch the other girls watching me. I can tell by their horrified expressions that I'm outta the club. But I don't really care.

I take my time to finish chewing, enjoying all the texture and flavor and everything that I've been missing. Ah, food is so good. Then I look back up at Thea and say, "All I know is that not eating was making me feel sick. My heart has been pounding pretty hard lately, and I have been really tired and — "

"That's because you're a beginner," says Thea, tossing a long, dark braid over her shoulder and glancing at the other Rexies for support. They just nod like obedient bobble-head dolls. "Once your body gets used to being deprived it will start to work — "

"Start to work?" I say, incredulously. "Or start to shut down? Let me tell you, I saw it with my own eyes, Lisa's body was shutting down last night. You can't starve yourself and expect to keep living." I'm practically shouting now, and I can tell the mess hall has gotten really, really quiet.

"Look," I say in a calmer voice, "it's your life, Thea, and if you want to live it in a constant state of starvation that may someday kill you, well, that's your choice." Then I stand up and pick up my tray. "But I'm not going to do it anymore." Then I turn and leave their table. And as I walk

away I can hear several people starting to clap, and soon it sounds like the whole room is clapping. And I am just stunned.

"Over here," calls Leah as she makes room at their table for me. "This is Jordan," she tells her friends. "The one who saved Lisa's life last night."

I love those who love me;
those who look for me find me.

Proverbs 8:17

Life on Purpose

Most people want their lives to have purpose. But God wants you to live purposely for him — and then he gives you the purpose. In other words, living for God is a daily thing. Sure, you can make your plan, and you can even design your life, but without making it that moment-by-moment, daily sort of commitment, you will probably fall flat on your face. Hey, you might fall on your face anyway. Everyone does from time to time.

But the difference between someone who flounders and someone who moves on is the willingness to admit your failures and learn from your mistakes. That's God's purpose for you — he knows you're not perfect and that you're going to blow it, but he wants you to bring your imperfections to him. He wants you to have an honest and humble heart, a willingness to experience his forgiveness and grace, and then share it with others around you. And when you begin to understand the simplicity of that purpose, you begin to live the kind of rewarding life that God intended for you — the kind of life that brings him glory!

Getting Honest

So, answer these questions:

4. How pleased do you think God is with your life? Why?

5. Do you feel that others can see God when they look at you? Why or why not?

6. Is there any part of your life that doesn't bring glory to God? If so, what?

7. What kind of message would you like God to send through you?

8. Are there others you think God can touch through your life? List them.

jordan's story ends . . .

It's the last day of camp and I can't believe it, but I'm seriously sad to leave. I've made some totally amazing friends here, including Leah and Amazon Girl and even Polly (who never calls me Babyfat anymore).

Our cabin of seven girls (after Lisa left) lost a total of 67½ pounds. Incredible! But there were cabins that lost even more weight. I guess maybe someone at fat camp knows what they're doing after all.

Besides making some cool friends, and actually learning a little about nutrition and exercise (since I was finally able to pay attention with some food in my stomach), I even lost a few pounds myself. Not as much as the other girls, but Amazon Girl said that's because I didn't have as much to lose. Apparently it's easier to lose more when you weigh more. Anyway, I don't really care about that as much anymore.

The biggest thing I learned is that you have to accept yourself for who you are. Because the truth is, you're never going to look "perfect." I mean, I'm short and a little stocky (Leah says I should call it muscular and I think she's right). But I'm also a good gymnast, a good cheerleader — and more importantly, I think I'm a good friend. And I do a mean case of CPR. Just ask Lisa.

She visited camp yesterday. Her parents brought her to pick up her things, and then they took me to lunch with them (where I ate all kinds of forbidden foods — it was great!). They thanked me for doing CPR and I told them about how I kept praying for her all night. And we even talked about the anorexia thing for a bit. Apparently Lisa had only been doing it for some time and her parents weren't even aware of it. I did notice that Lisa's mom was very thin and I had to wonder . . . but I didn't say anything.

Anyway, I told Lisa that I'd given it up and how the Rexies wouldn't even speak to me anymore. Then we promised to stay in touch through e-mail. And I'm hoping that I'll get to share some more stuff with her. Stuff that I'm still learning myself. Like the fact that God made me like this for a reason. And before I go trying to change everything, I better come to him first. Oh, yeah, I think that's what Kara told me before I ever came to camp. Oh, well, it just goes to show you that you really should listen to your friends sometimes. But listen to God first. Then you know you can't go too far wrong.

Your thoughts — how rare, how beautiful!
God, I'll never comprehend them!
I couldn't even begin to count them —
any more than I could count the sand of the sea.
Oh, let me rise in the morning and live always with you!
Psalm 139:17-18

What About This?

9. How do you think Jordan's experience at fat camp changed her?

10. Do you think Jordan's life impacted anyone (besides Lisa) at camp?

11. What would you say to Jordan now?

Love Is the Key

Do you ever stop to think about what draws you to God? Isn't it his love that encourages you to spend time with him? His enormous love that was personified by his forgiveness when he allowed his own son to die on the cross? As always, love really is the key. Whether it's you drawing closer to God or him drawing closer to you — love is the power that pulls you together. The same is true when you love others.

If you can learn to love the way God loves, unconditionally and totally, you will automatically draw people to him. That's his plan. And while it's simple, it's not always easy. In fact, loving others can be your biggest challenge. But, as with any challenge, God is ready and waiting to give you what you need to get there. You just need to ask him.

Words to Live By

(Consider memorizing one of these verses.)

Bless your enemies; no cursing under your breath.
Laugh with your happy friends when they're happy;
share tears when they're down. Get along with each other;
don't be stuck-up. Make friends with nobodies;
don't be the great somebody.
Romans 12:14-16

This is my command: Love one another the way I loved you.
This is the very best way to love.
Put your life on the line for your friends.
John 15:12-13

What About This?

12. Romans 12:14-16 has some excellent advice. Choose one line that really speaks to you. Now write down what you can do to make that verse part of your life.

13. List all the words you can think of that you associate with the word love.

14. John 15:12-13 is one of Jesus' biggest challenges to us. Write one way that you could "put your life on the line" for a friend.

15. Using one of your previous answers, create a goal that you think would bring glory to God in your life.

My Final Goals

Now it's time to go back over your other five lists of goals and put them together to make a composite list here. See if you can create one single goal for each section in the space provided below.

My Final Goals Are:

1. [I want to accept that God made me like this for a reason. I will thank him daily for my big nose.]

2. [I know that I'm a melancholic now and I want to practice being more positive and outgoing. I will smile at someone new every day.]

3. [I know that I've been spending too much time playing video games. I want to sculpt my soul into something that pleases God, so I commit to thirty minutes of reading the Bible a day.]

4. [I see that my perception of beauty is whacked out, so I'm throwing away my stack of glam rags and inviting God to do an extreme makeover on me.]

5. [I believe God has given me a natural talent for sports and a spiritual gift of encouragement, I want to use these to glorify him in track this season by cheering others on.]

6. [I want to live my life to glorify God. I will commit to a daily quiet time every morning at seven.]

Now that you've made these goals, post them someplace where you can check them on a regular basis.

All for Him

Have you ever seen a racehorse that's in top form? A beautiful, muscular thoroughbred that's been bred and trained to do one thing and one thing only — and that's to race. It's like that horse is only happy when he's doing just that — going full speed, running for the roses. It's what he was born to do.

In a way, you're like that too. God designed you with the need to give yourself wholeheartedly to him — so much so that you'll only be truly happy when you're doing that. He wants you to go strong and hard for him. And he'll give you what it takes to do it. In other words, God is sold out on you — he wants you to be sold out on him.

16. How satisfied are you with your life? Why is that?

17. What can you do to strengthen your commitment to God?

18. What do you think God is trying to tell you right now?

19. Use the space below to write a prayer of commitment and thanks.

"The person who trusts me will not only do what I'm doing but even greater things, because I, on my way to the Father, am giving you the same work to do that I've been doing. You can count on it. From now on, whatever you request along the lines of who I am and what I am doing, I'll do it. That's how the Father will be seen for who he is in the Son. I mean it. Whatever you request in this way, I'll do."

John 14:12-14

author

Melody Carlson has written dozens of books for all age groups, but she particularly enjoys writing for teens. Perhaps this is because her own teen years remain so vivid in her memory. After claiming to be an atheist at the ripe old age of twelve, she later surrendered her heart to Jesus and has been following him ever since. Her hope and prayer for all her readers is that each one would be touched by God in a special way through her stories. For more information, visit Melody's website at www.melodycarlson.com.